MEXICAN

C·O·O·K·I·N·G
Exciting Ideas for Delicious Meals

Photography by Peter Barry
Designed by Claire Leighton and
Helen Johnson
Edited by Jillian Stewart and Kate Cranshaw

3564
This edition published 1996 by Bramley Books
© Bramley Books, Godalming, Surrey
All rights reserved
Printed and bound in Hong Kong
ISBN 1-85833-549-3

MEXICAN
C·O·O·K·I·N·G
Exciting Ideas for Delicious Meals

Bramley Books

Contents

Introduction

Mexican cooking is a riot of flavour and colour. It is as flamboyant as the sombrero, as fiery as the Mexican sun, and has roots that go back to the Aztecs. The tastes are distinctive and never bland. The shapes are interesting too with many varying little parcels, rolls and envelopes filled with piquant surprises. Many of the favourite adopted dishes from Mexico originate in the street food stalls that line every Mexican thoroughfare. The little stuffed packets that are thrust at the passengers through train windows at Mexican railway stations become very acceptable dinner-party fare when dressed up with side-dishes of rice and salads of tomato and avocado.

In Mexico the tortilla is generally the base to all savoury foods, and is the wrapping that encloses the meat, vegetables, salad and cheese or whatever is locally available. Tortillas are basically unleavened rounds of maize bread. They are rolled into a flat pancake and baked on a hot griddle. Outside of Mexico it is more common to use wheat flour for making tortillas, as this produces an acceptable substitute which is easier to prepare than the corn variety. The tortilla is mentioned frequently in these recipes and appears in many different guises: for Enchiladas tortillas are filled, rolled, covered with a sauce and then baked; for Chimichangas tortillas are filled and then fried; and for Tacos the tortillas are first fried and then filled.

These plain, unleavened bread bases are used as a foil for the sharp and fiery all-Mexican tastes of chillies, green peppers, spring onions, lime juice and garlic. These are the key ingredients without which the end effect is not authentic. Of course, all these can be adjusted to suit individual tastes. Chillies in particular do vary in strength and should be used with some caution. To scale down their heat, remove the inner core of seeds and pith, but if you enjoy them hot, just chop them up and toss them in. Be careful not to touch your eyes after chopping chillies and wash your hands thoroughly. They are powerful beasts!

Cocoa is another important Mexican ingredient which appears surprisingly in some savoury dishes. It is not used as a sweetening but as a seasoning as was traditional in pre-Columbian Mexico. You do not notice a chocolate flavour in these dishes, the cocoa rather adds a depth and richness to the sauce. Cocoa is native to southern Mexico and was imported by the Aztecs into central Mexico where it was so valued they used cocoa beans as a form of currency. Later it was used to make chocolate – an Aztec word – which they drank as a stimulating, energy-rich drink. Cinnamon, which is often combined with chocolate in Mexican recipes, is also a traditional Mexican spice.

If you are not familiar with Mexican cooking, then embrace it as an uncomplicated and stimulating new addition to your culinary repertoire.

CORNMEAL PANCAKES

Cornmeal, either yellow, white or blue, is an important ingredient in Mexican recipes. Here it's combined with sweetcorn in a light and unusual starter.

SERVES 4

150g/5oz yellow cornmeal
1 tbsp flour
1 tsp baking powder
1 tsp salt
2 eggs, separated
460ml/16 fl oz buttermilk
Oil
275g/10oz frozen sweetcorn, defrosted
Red Pepper Relish (see recipe)
Spring onions, chopped
Soured cream

1. Sift the dry ingredients into a bowl, adding any coarse meal that remains in the sieve.

2. Mix the egg yolks and buttermilk together and gradually beat into the dry ingredients. Cover and leave to stand for at least 15 minutes.

3. Whisk the egg whites until stiff but not dry and fold into the cornmeal mixture.

4. Lightly grease a frying pan with oil and drop in about 2 tbsps of the batter. Sprinkle with some of the sweetcorn and allow to cook until the underside is golden brown. Turn the pancakes and cook the second side until golden. Cook three or four pancakes at once. Keep the cooked pancakes warm.

5. To serve, place three pancakes on warm side plates. Add a spoonful of soured cream and Red Pepper Relish to each and sprinkle over finely sliced or shredded spring onions.

TIME: Preparation takes about 30 minutes, including standing time for the batter. Cooking takes about 3-4 minutes per batch of pancakes.

COOK'S TIP: Allowing the pancake batter to stand 15 minutes before using it will produce a batter that is lighter and easier to use. This standing time also helps the cornmeal to soften.

SERVING IDEAS: Serve as a starter with the accompaniments or serve alone as a side dish to a main course.

CHILLI VEGETABLE SOUP

This delicious soup makes a light first course.

SERVES 4

1 tbsp oil
1 onion, chopped
120g/4oz canned whole green chillies,
    quartered
850ml/1½ pints chicken stock
1 large potato, peeled and cut into short
    sticks
Full quantity Taco Sauce recipe
1 tbsp lime juice
Salt
Tortilla chips and lime slices, to garnish

1. Heat the oil in a large saucepan and sauté the onion until translucent. Add the green chillies, stock, potato and taco sauce.

2. Cover the pan and simmer the soup for 20 minutes. Stir in the lime juice and add salt to taste.

3. Serve in individual bowls with tortilla chips. Cut a thin slice of lime to float in each bowl of soup.

TIME: Preparation takes about 20 minutes and cooking takes 20 minutes.

VARIATION: Use only half a can green chillies if wished, or cook green peppers with the onions instead.

SERVING IDEAS: For a more filling soup, add some cooked rice.

GUACAMOLE

This is one of Mexico's most famous dishes. It is delicious as a first course on its own or as an ingredient in other recipes.

SERVES 8

1 medium onion, finely chopped
1 clove garlic, crushed
Grated zest and juice ½ lime
½ quantity Taco Sauce (see recipe)
3 large ripe avocados
1 tbsp chopped fresh coriander
Salt and black pepper
Coriander leaves, to garnish
Tortilla chips, to serve

1. Mix the onion, garlic, zest and juice of the lime and the taco sauce together in a large bowl.

2. Cut the avocados in half lengthwise. Twist the halves gently in opposite directions to separate.

3. Hit the stone with the blade of a large, sharp knife and twist the knife to remove the stone.

4. Place the avocado halves cut side down on a chopping board. Lightly score the skin lengthwise and gently pull back to peel. Alternatively, scoop out avocado flesh with a spoon, scraping the skin well.

5. Chop the avocado roughly and immediately place in the bowl with the onion and lime.

6. Use a potato masher to break up the avocado until almost smooth. Do not over-mash. Season, and stir in the chopped coriander. Spoon into a serving bowl and garnish with coriander leaves.

7. Surround the bowl with tortilla chips for dipping.

TIME: Preparation takes about 25 minutes.

PREPARATION: Do not prepare too long in advance. The avocado will darken even with the addition of lime juice if left too long.

COOK'S TIP: Try leaving the avocado stone in the mixture. This is said to delay discolouration.

PRAWNS ACAPULCO

These make a stylish starter or a quickly prepared snack. Make the bread slices smaller to serve with cocktails.

SERVES 4

---

4 slices bread, crusts removed
90g/3oz softened butter
175g/6oz cooked and peeled prawns
½ tsp chilli powder
¼ tsp paprika
½ tsp cumin
Salt and pepper
Watercress, to garnish

1. Cut the bread slices in half and spread each side sparingly with 30g/1oz of the butter.

2. Place the bread on a baking tray and cook in a preheated oven at 180°C/350°F/ Gas Mark 4, for 10-15 minutes until golden brown and crisp. Keep warm.

3. Melt the remaining butter in a small pan and stir in the prawns, spices and seasoning.

4. Heat through completely and spoon on top of the bread slices. Garnish with watercress and serve hot.

TIME: Preparation takes about 15 minutes. The bread will take 15-20 minutes to cook until golden, and the prawns take about 5 minutes to heat through.

WATCHPOINT: Do not heat the prawns too long or at too high a temperature as they toughen easily.

COOK'S TIP: The bread may be prepared in advance and reheated for 5 minutes in the oven. Do not reheat the prawns.

BEEF & BEAN SOUP

In Mexico, the day's main meal is eaten at around 2.00 pm and this soup is a popular starter.

SERVES 4

1 large onion, finely chopped
1 red pepper, finely chopped
2 sticks celery, chopped
2 tbsps oil
225g/8oz minced beef
6 tomatoes, skinned, seeded and chopped
430g/15oz can refried beans
1 tsp ground cumin
1 tsp chilli powder
Pinch of cinnamon and cayenne pepper
1 tsp crushed garlic
Salt and pepper
420ml/¾ pint beef stock

1. Sauté the onion, pepper and celery in the oil in a large saucepan until softened.

2. Add the beef and fry over a medium heat until well browned. Add the tomatoes and refried beans with the spices, garlic and seasoning. Mix well.

3. Stir in the stock and bring to the boil. Cover and simmer gently for 30 minutes, stirring occasionally.

4. Pour the soup into a blender or food processor and purée. The soup should be quite thick and not completely smooth.

5. Adjust the seasoning and serve with tortilla chips. Top with some soured cream if wished.

TIME: Preparation takes about 20 minutes and cooking takes about 50 minutes.

PREPARATION: Purée the soup in 2 or 3 small batches.

TO FREEZE: Allow the puréed soup to cool completely and skim any fat from the surface. Pour into freezer containers, label and freeze for up to 3 months.

CEVICHE

In this traditional Mexican dish the raw fish is 'cooked' in a mixture of oil and lime juice. Quick and easy to prepare, ceviche makes a highly nutritious and very tasty starter.

SERVES 4

460g/1lb fresh cod fillet, skinned
Juice and grated zest of 2 limes
1 small shallot, finely chopped
1 green chilli, seeded and finely chopped
1 tsp ground coriander
1 small green pepper, sliced
1 small red pepper, sliced
4 spring onions, finely chopped
1 tbsp fresh parsley, chopped
1 tbsp fresh coriander, chopped
2 tbsps olive oil
Freshly ground black pepper
1 small lettuce, to serve

1. Using a sharp knife cut the fish into very thin strips across the grain. Put the strips into a large bowl and pour over the lime juice.

2. Stir in the grated lime zest, shallot, chilli and ground coriander. Mix well.

3. Cover the bowl with cling film and refrigerate for 24 hours, stirring occasionally during this time to ensure that the fish remains well coated in the lime.

4. Mix the sliced peppers, spring onions and the fresh herbs together in a large bowl.

5. Put the fish mixture into a colander and drain off the juice.

6. Put the drained fish into the pepper mixture and stir in the oil, mixing well to coat evenly. Add freshly ground pepper to taste.

7. Finely shred the lettuce and arrange on a serving plate. Spread the fish mixture attractively over the lettuce and serve immediately, garnished with slices of lime, if wished.

TIME: Preparation takes 20 minutes, plus 24 hours standing time.

VARIATION: Use hake or salmon in place of the cod in this recipe.

SERVING IDEAS: As well as being an interesting starter, Ceviche can also be served with tortillas for a tasty lunch.

SALAD HUEVOS RANCHEROS

Rancheros egg salad makes excellent lunch or brunch fare.

SERVES 4

2 large red peppers, roasted (see Chicken with Red Peppers)

2 chorizo sausages, blanched and cut into thin strips

4 heads chicory

1 large or 2 small courgettes, cut into matchstick pieces

1 small jicama root, cut into matchstick pieces

4 spring onions, shredded

30g/4 tbsps pine nuts

4 eggs

Dressing

1 tsp chopped fresh coriander

90ml/6 tbsps oil

2 tbsps lime juice

Dash of Tabasco

Salt and pinch of sugar

1. Prepare the roasted peppers and cut it into thin strips. Blanch the chorizo as for Indian Bread Chorizo and Salsa.

2. Separate the leaves of the chicory and slice or leave whole if small.

3. Bring a pan of water to the boil and blanch the courgette and jicama strips for 1 minute. Rinse under cold water until completely cool and leave to drain. Combine with the chicory and spring onions. Add the strips of chorizo and set aside.

4. Toast the pine nuts, in a small roasting tin, under a moderate grill, for about 5 minutes or until golden brown. Stir often to prevent burning.

5. Bring at least 5cm/2 inches of water to the boil in a large frying pan. Turn down the heat to simmering. Break one of the eggs onto a saucer or into a cup.

6. Stir the water to make a whirlpool and then carefully pour the egg into the centre, keeping the saucer or cup close to the level of the water. When the water stops swirling and the white begins to set, gently move the egg over to the side of the pan and repeat with each remaining egg. Cook the eggs until the whites are completely set, but the yolks are still soft.

7. Remove the eggs from the water with a draining spoon and place them immediately into a bowl of cold water.

8. Mix the dressing ingredients together and pour half over all the vegetables and sausage. Toss to coat. Arrange the mixture on individual plates in the shape of nests.

9. Remove the eggs from the cold water with the draining spoon and hold them over a towel for a few minutes to drain completely. Place one egg in the middle of each nest. Spoon the remaining dressing over each egg, sprinkle over the pine nuts and garnish the yolk with a coriander leaf.

TIME: Preparation takes about 45 minutes and cooking takes about 5 minutes for the eggs, 1 minute to blanch the vegetables and 10 minutes to blanch the chorizo.
BUYING GUIDE: Jicama, also known as the yam bean is available from ethnic food stores. If unavailable substitute a small can of water chestnuts.

MEXICAN BEEF PATTIES

Refried beans added to the meat mixture make moist and tasty beefburgers that are slightly out of the ordinary.

SERVES 4

1 tbsp oil
1 onion, finely chopped
340g/12oz minced beef
225g/8oz canned refried beans
15g/4 tbsps breadcrumbs
½ tsp cumin
1 tsp chilli powder
1 clove garlic, crushed
Salt and pepper
1 egg, beaten
Flour to coat
Oil for frying
Watercress, to garnish

1. Heat the oil in a saucepan, add the onion and sauté until soft but not browned. Remove from the heat and mix into the beef, beans, breadcrumbs, spices, garlic and seasoning in a bowl, gradually adding the egg until the mixture holds together well.

2. Turn the mixture out onto a well floured surface and divide into 8 pieces.

3. Shape into even-sized patties with well floured hands. Knead the pieces before shaping, if necessary, to make sure mixture holds together with no cracks.

4. Coat lightly with flour and refrigerate until firm.

5. Pour enough oil into a large frying pan to completely cover the patties. Fry two at a time until golden brown on all sides and completely cooked through.

6. Remove from the oil and drain on kitchen paper. Arrange on a serving plate and garnish with watercress.

TIME: Preparation takes about 20 minutes plus at least 1 hour's refrigeration. Cooking takes about 30 minutes.

PREPARATION: If the mixture is too soft to shape, add 2 tbsps flour.

SERVING IDEAS: Serve with soured cream or taco sauce and an avocado and tomato salad. Accompany with warm flour tortillas.

TO FREEZE: The meat patties can be made up ahead of time and frozen on baking trays until firm. Place in rigid containers with waxed paper between each patty. Defrost in the refrigerator before cooking. Do not use mince that has been previously frozen.

MEXICAN CHICKEN & PEPPER SALAD

This is the perfect lunch or light supper dish during the summer, and it can be prepared in advance.

SERVES 6

460g/1lb cooked chicken, cut in strips
60ml/2 fl oz mayonnaise
60ml/2 fl oz natural yogurt
1 tsp chilli powder
1 tsp paprika
Pinch cayenne pepper
½ tsp tomato purée
1 tsp onion purée
1 green pepper, finely sliced
1 red pepper, finely sliced
175g/6oz frozen sweetcorn, defrosted
175g/6oz long grain rice, cooked

1. Place the chicken strips in a large mixing bowl.

2. Mix the mayonnaise, yogurt, spices, tomato and onion purées together and leave to stand briefly for the flavours to blend. Fold the dressing into the chicken.

3. Add the peppers and sweetcorn and mix gently until all the ingredients are coated with the dressing.

4. Place the rice on a serving dish and pile the salad into the centre. Serve immediately.

TIME: Preparation takes about 30 minutes.

PREPARATION: Chicken salad may be prepared several hours in advance and kept covered in the refrigerator. Spoon onto the rice just before serving.

VARIATION: Add sliced or diced green chillies or Jalapeno peppers for a hotter flavour. Try chilli sauce or taco sauce as an alternative seasoning.

BUYING GUIDE: Onion purée is available in tubes like tomato purée.

INDIAN BREAD WITH CHORIZO AND SALSA

A version of this bread has been baked by American Indians for generations.

SERVES 4-6

Bread
225g/8oz plain flour
1 tbsp baking powder
Pinch salt
15g/½oz vegetable shortening
2 tsps cumin seeds
200ml/7 fl oz water
Oil, for deep-fat frying

Chorizo topping
2 medium red potatoes
460g/1lb chorizo sausage
4 spring onions, chopped

Salsa
1 clove garlic
30g/1oz coriander leaves
1 tsp fresh oregano
Half or less fresh red or green chilli, seeded
Pinch salt and mustard powder
Juice of 2 limes
175ml/6 fl oz oil
Shredded lettuce, crumbled goat's cheese
    and chopped tomatoes, to garnish

1. Sift the flour, baking powder and salt into a bowl. Rub in the shortening and then stir in the cumin seeds. Stir in enough of the water to make a soft, slightly sticky dough. Knead several times, cover and leave to stand for 15-20 minutes.

2. Divide the dough into 8 pieces and roll or pat into 12.5cm/5-inch circles on a well floured surface. Make a hole in the centre of each with your finger and leave the circles to stand, covered, for 30 minutes.

3. Meanwhile, boil the potatoes in their skins in a covered saucepan. Place the chorizo in a pan and cover with water. Cover the pan and bring to the boil. Lower the heat and simmer for about 10 minutes, or until just tender. Remove the chorizo from the water and peel off the casings while the sausage is still warm. Chop sausage roughly and set aside. When the potatoes are tender, drain them and leave to cool. Cut the potatoes into 1.25cm/½-inch dice.

4. To prepare the salsa, place the garlic, coriander, oregano, chilli, salt and mustard into a food processor and add the lime juice. Process until well blended. With the machine running, pour in the oil in a thin, steady stream. Process until smooth and adjust the seasoning.

5. Pour some oil into a deep-fat fryer to a depth of about 5-7.5cm/2-3 inches. Heat to 190°C/375°F. Carefully lower in one dough circle and push it underneath the oil with a large metal spoon. Fry for about 30 seconds, turn over and fry the other side. Drain each while frying the others.

6. Mix the chorizo, spring onions and potatoes with enough of the salsa to moisten. Arrange the lettuce on top of the bread and spoon on the chorizo topping. Spoon on any remaining salsa, sprinkle with the tomato and cheese.

TIME: Preparation takes 50 minutes. Cooking takes 30 minutes.

MOYETTES

While these sandwiches make excellent lunch fare, they are very popular for breakfast in Mexico.

SERVES 4

4 crusty rolls
30g/1oz butter or margarine
225g/8oz canned refried beans
2 spring onions, chopped
30g/4 tbsps grated Tilsit cheese

1. Cut the rolls in half and remove some of the inside.

2. Soften the butter and spread on the insides of the rolls.

3. Fill the bottom halves of the rolls with the refried beans.

4. Sprinkle with the spring onion and top with the grated cheese then the bread 'lids'.

5. Place the rolls on a baking sheet and cook in an oven preheated to 160°C/325°F/Gas Mark 3, for 15-20 minutes, or until the cheese has melted and the beans are hot. Serve immediately.

TIME: Preparation takes about 15 minutes and cooking takes about 15-20 minutes.

COOK'S TIP: The Moyettes may be prepared in advance and heated through just before serving. Once heated, they do not reheat successfully.

VARIATION: Use red onion and Cheddar, or Monterey Jack cheese if available.

CHILLI PRAWN QUICHE

Fresh chillies give a Mexican flavour to this prawn-filled quiche.

SERVES 6

Pastry
120g/4oz plain flour
Pinch of salt
30g/1oz butter or margarine
30g/1oz white cooking fat
30-60ml/2-4 tbsps cold water

Filling
4 eggs
120ml/4 fl oz milk
120ml/4 fl oz single cream
Salt
½ clove garlic, crushed
120g/4oz Cheddar cheese, grated
3 spring onions, chopped
2 green chillies, seeded and chopped
225g/8oz cooked and peeled prawns
Cooked, unpeeled prawns and parsley
    sprigs, for garnish

1. Sieve the flour with the salt into a mixing bowl, or place in a food processor and mix once or twice.

2. Rub in the butter and fat until the mixture resembles fine breadcrumbs, or work in the food processor, being careful not to over-mix.

3. Mix in the water gradually, adding enough to bring the pastry together into a ball. If using a food processor, add the water through the feed tube while the machine is running.

4. Wrap the pastry well and chill for 20-30 minutes.

5. Roll the pastry out, on a well floured surface to a circle large enough to line a 25cm/10-inch flan ring.

6. Mix the eggs, milk, cream, salt and garlic together. Sprinkle the cheese, onion, chillies and prawns onto the base of the pastry and pour over the egg mixture.

7. Bake in an oven preheated to 200°C/400°F/Gas Mark 6, for 30-40 minutes until firm and golden brown. Peel the tail shells off the whole prawns and remove the legs. Use to garnish the quiche along with the sprigs of parsley.

TIME: Preparation takes about 40 minutes, including chilling. Cooking takes 30-40 minutes.

VARIATION: Add diced red or green peppers and chopped coriander leaves to the filling before baking.

SERVING IDEAS: Serve hot or cold with a salad for a light meal. Serve as a starter, cut in thin wedges or baked in individual dishes.

EMPANADAS (SAVOURY TURNOVERS)

These turnovers are very popular throughout Latin America.

MAKES 6

Triple quantity pastry recipe from Chilli
    Prawn Quiche

1 egg

Filling

1 onion, chopped

1 clove garlic, finely chopped

1 small green pepper, chopped

1 tbsp oil

225g/8oz minced beef

1 tsp cocoa powder

1 tbsp flour

½ tsp ground cumin

½ tsp paprika

½ tsp dried oregano, crushed

Salt and pepper

1-2 chillies, seeded and chopped

2 tbsps tomato purée

3 tbsps water

2 tbsps flaked almonds

2 tbsps raisins

1. Prepare the pastry according to the recipe for Chilli Prawn Quiche.

2. Cook the onion, garlic and green pepper in the oil until soft but not coloured. Add the meat and fry quickly until well browned.

3. Add the cocoa, flour, spices, oregano and seasoning. Stir well and cook briefly before adding the chillies, tomato purée and water. Cook slowly for 10-15 minutes, then add the nuts and raisins and allow to cool.

4. Roll the pastry out on a floured surface and cut out 6 rounds using a 15cm/6-inch plate or saucepan lid as a guide.

5. Place the cooled filling on one half of each pastry round and dampen the edges with water.

6. Fold over and press the edges together to seal, crimping them if wished.

7. Place the turnovers on baking sheets and brush with some beaten egg mixed with a little salt. Make sure the egg glaze is brushed on evenly.

8. Prick the turnovers once or twice with a fork and bake in an oven preheated to 220°C/425°F/Gas Mark 7, for about 15 minutes or until golden brown.

TIME: Preparation takes about 30 minutes, plus 30 minutes chilling. Cooking takes about 20 minutes for the filling and about 15 minutes for the turnovers.

PREPARATION: The turnovers may be baked in advance and reheated for about 5 minutes in a hot oven before serving. They may also be served cold.

SERVING IDEAS: Serve hot or cold as a light meal accompanied with a salad. Empanadas are perfect for picnics.

NACHOS

These make excellent cocktail savouries and the variety of toppings and flavour combinations is almost endless.

SERVES 8-10

Beef filling

2 tsps oil
225g/8oz minced beef
2 tsps chilli powder
Pinch of ground coriander
Pinch of cayenne pepper
Salt and pepper

1 pack round tortilla chips
1 can refried beans
Full quantity Taco Sauce recipe
1 can Jalapeño bean dip
8-10 cherry tomatoes, sliced
120ml/4 fl oz soured cream or natural
    yogurt
Black and stuffed green olives, sliced
Cheddar cheese, grated

1. Heat the oil for the beef filling in a frying pan and brown the mince, breaking the meat up as it cooks. Add the spices and seasoning and cook for about 20 minutes.

2. Top half of the tortilla chips with the refried beans and half with the beef filling.

3. Place a spoonful of taco sauce on the bean-topped chips and Jalapeño bean dip on the beef-topped chips.

4. Top the tortilla chips with tomatoes, soured cream or yogurt, olives or cheese in any combination, and serve.

TIME: Preparation takes about 25 minutes.

VARIATION: If wished, heat through for 5 minutes in a moderate oven before topping with tomatoes, soured cream or olives. Cheese may be sprinkled on to melt before serving.

COOK'S TIP: Tortilla chips will become slightly soggy if topped too soon before serving.

CHIMICHANGAS

A strange sounding name for a delicious snack which is something like a deep-fried taco.

SERVES 6

6 tortillas (see recipe for Flour Tortillas)
Half quantity Chilli Con Carne recipe
6 lettuce leaves, shredded
6 spring onions, chopped
90g/3oz Cheddar cheese, grated
Oil, for frying
Half quantity Guacamole recipe
140ml/¼ pint soured cream
1 tomato, seeded and chopped

1. Wrap the tortillas in foil and place in a warm oven for 5 minutes to make them pliable.

2. Heat the chilli briefly and spoon about 2 tbsps onto the centre of each tortilla. Top with the lettuce, spring onions and cheese.

3. Fold in the sides to make a parcel, making sure all the filling is enclosed.

4. Heat about 2.5cm/1 inch of oil in a large frying pan and when hot, lower in the chimichangas folded side down first. Cook 2-4 at a time depending on the size of the pan.

5. Cook for 3 minutes and carefully turn over. Cook a further 3 minutes, remove to kitchen paper and drain. Repeat with remaining chimichangas.

6. Spoon the guacamole over the top of each and drizzle over the soured cream. Sprinkle over the chopped tomato and serve immediately.

TIME: Preparation takes about 30 minutes. This does not include time to prepare the tortillas or the chilli. Cooking time for the chimichangas is about 12-18 minutes.

PREPARATION: Tortillas and chilli con carne can be made in advance and the chimichangas cooked just before serving. They do not reheat successfully.

SERVING IDEAS: Serve with rice and refried beans.

CHALUPAS

These are tortillas in another form, this time a snack with spicy meat. Create your own combination with a selection of different toppings.

MAKES 10

Half quantity tortilla recipe (see Fruit
    Empanada recipe)
Oil, for frying

Red sauce
60ml/4 tbsps oil
1 medium onion, finely chopped
1-2 green chillies, finely chopped
1-2 cloves garlic, crushed
8 fresh ripe tomatoes, skinned, seeded and
    chopped
6 sprigs fresh coriander, chopped
3 tbsps tomato purée

Meat sauce
340g/12oz minced beef
2 cloves garlic, crushed
1 tsp dried oregano
2 tsps cumin
Salt and pepper
90g/3oz frozen sweetcorn, defrosted
45g/4 tbsps raisins

Toppings
6-8 spring onions, chopped
4-6 tomatoes, diced
½ small head lettuce, shredded
120ml/4 fl oz soured cream
120g/4oz cheese, grated

1. Prepare the tortillas according to the recipe and divide the dough in 10. After the required resting time, roll the balls of dough out into 9cm/3½-inch rounds.

2. To prepare the red sauce, heat the oil in a large saucepan, add the onion, chillies and garlic, and cook to soften but not brown. Add the rest of the sauce ingredients, and simmer for about 15 minutes. Purée in a food processor or blender until smooth, then set aside.

3. Heat at least 5cm/2 inches of oil in a frying pan or medium saucepan. When hot, place in one tortilla and fry briefly until just crisp. Fry one at a time. Drain and keep warm.

4. To make the meat sauce, cook the beef slowly until the fat begins to render. Add the garlic, oregano and cumin and raise the heat to brown the meat. Season to taste and then stir in enough of the red sauce to moisten the meat well. Add the sweetcorn and raisins, cover the pan and leave to stand for 5 minutes.

5. Spoon the meat onto the tortillas and drizzle over more red sauce. Garnish with your choice of toppings.

TIME: Preparation takes about 40 minutes and cooking takes about 30 seconds for the tortillas, 15 minutes for the sauce and about 15 minutes to finish the beef topping.

CHEESE OR VEGETABLE ENCHILADAS

Choose between these fillings for a vegetarian version of Enchiladas.

SERVES 4

8 Tortillas (see recipe for Fruit Empanadas)
Full quantity Red Sauce (see Chalupas recipe)
Full quantity Mole Verde (see Gulf Coast Tacos)

Cheese filling
2 tbsps oil
1 small red pepper, finely diced
1 clove garlic, crushed
1 tbsp chopped fresh coriander
120ml/4 fl oz double cream
120g/4oz cream cheese
60g/2oz mild cheese, grated
Whole coriander leaves

Vegetable filling
2 tbsps oil
1 small onion, finely chopped
1 green pepper, diced
2 courgettes, diced
½ tsp oregano
½ tsp ground cumin
120g/4oz sweetcorn, fresh or frozen
Salt and pepper
175g/6oz grated mild cheese
Soured cream

1. Prepare the tortillas, red sauce and mole verde according to the recipe directions.

2. Heat a lightly oiled, heavy-based frying pan over a high heat. Carefully place in a tortilla and cook for about 1½ minutes, per side, or until bubbles form on the surface. Stack and cover with foil until all are cooked, keeping them warm in an oven until ready to be used.

3. Heat the oil for the cheese filling and cook the pepper and garlic slowly to soften. Add the coriander and pour in the cream. Bring to the boil and cook rapidly to thicken. Add the cream cheese and stir to melt. Add the grated cheese, stir in and keep the filling warm.

4. Place one tortilla at a time on serving dishes and spoon in the cheese filling. Fold over both sides to the middle. Re-heat the red sauce, if necessary, and spoon over the centre of two enchiladas. Garnish with coriander leaves.

5. For the vegetable filling, heat the oil and cook the onion to soften. Add the pepper, courgettes, oregano and cumin and cook for about 3 minutes or until the onions are soft. Add the sweetcorn, heat through and season to taste. Stir in the cheese and fill the tortillas as before, but place in a baking dish. Cook, covered, in an oven preheated to 180°C/350°F/Gas Mark 4, for about 10-15 minutes, or until the cheese has melted and the filling is beginning to bubble. Serve topped with soured cream and mole verde.

TIME: Preparation takes about 1 hour. Cheese filling takes about 10 minutes to cook and the vegetable filling takes 13-18 minutes.

BURRITOS

The name Burritos means 'little donkeys' and this dish is a very popular one.
Beans are the traditional filling, but meat may be used as well.

SERVES 6

6 tortillas (see recipe for Flour Tortillas)
1 onion, chopped
1 tbsp oil
460g/1lb canned refried beans
6 lettuce leaves, shredded
120g/4oz Cheddar cheese, grated
2 tomatoes, sliced
2 tbsps snipped chives
Full quantity Taco Sauce recipe
140ml/¼ pint soured cream
Chopped coriander leaves

1. Wrap the tortillas in foil and heat in a warm oven to soften.

2. Cook the onion in the oil until soft but not coloured. Add the beans and heat through.

3. Spoon the mixture down the centre of each tortilla. Top with the lettuce, cheese, tomatoes and chives. Fold over the sides to form long rectangular parcel. Make sure the filling is completely enclosed.

4. Place the burritos in an ovenproof dish, cover and cook in an oven preheated to 180°C/350°F/Gas Mark 4, for about 20 minutes.

5. Spoon over the taco sauce. Top with the soured cream and sprinkle with chopped coriander to serve.

TIME: Preparation takes about 25 minutes, not including making the tortillas. Cooking takes about 20 minutes.

PREPARATION: Heat just before serving. Burritos do not reheat well. Add extra chilli to the taco sauce recipe if wished.

SERVING IDEAS: Serve with rice and guacamole.

Tostadas

*These are popular all over Mexico and the toppings reflect the food available in
each area. They are delicious, but difficult to eat!*

MAKES 12

2 tsps oil
460g/1lb minced beef or pork
2 tsps chilli powder
1 tsp ground cumin
1 tsp ground coriander
1 can refried beans
1 pack tostada shells

Toppings
Shredded lettuce
Grated Cheddar cheese
Tomatoes, seeded and chopped
Soured cream
Olives
Cooked, peeled prawns
Spring onions, chopped
Taco Sauce (see recipe)

1. Heat the oil in a medium frying pan. Add the mince and fry quickly to brown then cook over a moderate heat for 8-10 minutes. Sprinkle on the spices and cook for 1-2 minutes.

2. Reheat the beans and place the tostada shells on a baking sheet. Heat for 2-3 minutes in a moderate oven.

3. Spread 1-2 tbsps of the beans on each tostada shell.

4. Top each shell with some of the beef mixture.

5. Add the topping ingredients in different combinations and serve immediately.

TIME: Preparation takes about 40 minutes, cooking takes about
10-15 minutes.

PREPARATION: All the ingredients can be prepared ahead of time. The
tostadas cannot be reheated once assembled.

VARIATION: Add chopped green or red peppers to the list of toppings
along with chopped green chillies or Jalapeño peppers and Guacamole.

GULF COAST TACOS

Around the Gulf of Mexico, ever popular tacos take on a new look and taste with a seafood filling.

SERVES 6

6 Tortillas (see recipe for Fruit Empanadas)
Oil, for deep frying

Mole verde
3 green tomatillos
1 tbsp oil
1 clove garlic, roughly chopped
30g/1oz coriander, roughly chopped
2 green chillies, roughly chopped
Juice of 1 lime
140ml/¼ pint soured cream
Pinch of salt and sugar

Filling ingredients
225g/8oz large raw prawns, peeled
225g/8oz raw scallops, quartered if large
1 tsp coriander seed, crushed
1 shallot, finely chopped
Salt and pepper
90ml/6 tbsps white wine
Water
1 small jicama, peeled and cut into thin
    matchstick strips
Coriander leaves and lime wedges

1. Prepare the Tortillas according to the recipe.

2. To make the mole verde, remove the papery husks from the tomatillos, and slice the flesh. Heat the oil in a small frying pan and sauté them for about 3 minutes, to soften. Place in a food processor along with the garlic, coriander, chillies and lime juice. Purée until smooth. Fold in the soured cream, adjust the seasoning and chill.

3. Heat some oil in a deep frying pan to a depth of at least 5cm/2 inches. When hot, place in a tortilla and press down under the oil with a metal spoon. When the tortilla starts to puff up, take it out and immediately fold in half to form a shell. Hold in shape until it cools slightly and sets. Repeat with the remaining tortillas. Keep them warm in an oven, standing on their open ends.

4. Place the prawns, scallops, coriander seeds, shallot and salt and pepper in a frying pan with the wine and just enough water to barely cover. Cook for about 8 minutes, stirring occasionally. The prawns should turn pink and the scallops will look opaque when cooked.

5. Fill each of the taco shells with some of the jicama. Remove the seafood from the liquid with a draining spoon and arrange on top of the jicama. Top with the mole verde and decorate with coriander leaves. Serve with lime wedges.

TIME: Preparation takes about 1 hour, including the time to make the tortillas.

BUYING GUIDE: Tomatillos, related to physalis, and jicama are only available in some specialist food shops. Use 1 large green tomato and a small tin of water chestnuts as a substitute.

ENCHILADAS

Although fillings and sauces vary, enchiladas (stuffed rolled tortillas) are one of the tastiest Mexican dishes. Serve with guacamole and/or refried beans.

SERVES 6

10 ripe tomatoes, skinned, seeded and chopped
1 small onion, chopped
1-2 green or red chillies, seeded and chopped
1 clove garlic, crushed
Salt
Pinch sugar
1-2 tbsps tomato purée
30g/1oz butter or margarine
2 eggs
225ml/8 fl oz double cream
340g/12oz minced pork
1 small red pepper, chopped
45g/4 tbsps raisins
30g/4 tbsps pine nuts
Salt and pepper
12 prepared tortillas (see recipe for Flour Tortillas)
30g/4 tbsps grated cheese
Sliced spring onions, to garnish

1. Place the tomatoes, onion, chillies, garlic, salt and sugar and tomato purée into a blender or food processor and purée until smooth.

2. Melt butter or margarine in a large saucepan. Add the puréed vegetables and simmer for 5 minutes.

3. Beat together the eggs and cream, mixing well. Add a spoonful of the hot purée to the cream and eggs and mix quickly. Return the mixture to the saucepan with the rest of the purée.

4. Heat slowly, stirring constantly, until the mixture thickens. Do not boil.

5. While preparing the sauce, cook the pork and pepper slowly in a large frying pan. Use a fork to break up the meat as it cooks. Turn up the heat when the pork is nearly cooked and fry briskly for a few minutes. Add the raisins, pine nuts and seasoning.

6. Combine about ¼ of the sauce with the meat and divide the mixture evenly among all the tortillas. Spoon the filling onto one side of the centre and roll up the tortillas around it, leaving the ends open and some of the filling showing.

7. Place the enchiladas seam side down in a baking dish and pour over the remaining sauce, leaving the ends uncovered. Sprinkle over the cheese and bake in an oven preheated to 180°C/350°F/Gas Mark 4, for 15-20 minutes, or until the sauce begins to bubble. Sprinkle with the sliced spring onions and serve immediately.

TIME: Preparation takes about 60 minutes to make the tortillas and about 30 minutes more to finish the dish.

WATCHPOINT: When preparing the sauce, do not allow it to boil or it will curdle.

TACOS

Ready made taco shells make this famous Mexican snack easy to prepare.

MAKES 12

---

12 taco shells

Beef filling
1 tbsp oil
460g/1lb minced beef
1 medium onion, chopped
2 tsps ground cumin
2 tsps chilli powder
Pinch of paprika
1 clove garlic, crushed
Salt and pepper

Chicken filling
45g/1½oz butter or margarine
1 medium onion, chopped
1 small red pepper, chopped
2 tbsps flaked almonds
340g/12oz chicken breasts, skinned and
    finely chopped
Salt and pepper
1 piece fresh ginger, peeled and chopped
90ml/6 tbsps milk
2 tsps cornflour
120ml/4 fl oz soured cream

Toppings
Shredded lettuce
Grated cheese
Tomatoes, seeded and chopped
Chopped spring onions
Avocado, sliced
Soured cream
Jalapeño peppers
Taco Sauce (see recipe)

1. Heat the oil for the beef filling in a large frying pan and brown the mince and onion, breaking the meat up as it cooks. Add the spices, garlic and seasoning and cook for about 20 minutes, then set aside.

2. For the chicken filling, melt 30g/1oz of the butter in a medium saucepan and add the onion. Cook slowly until softened.

3. Add the red pepper and almonds and cook slowly until the nuts are lightly browned. Stir often during cooking. Remove to a plate and set aside.

4. Melt the remaining butter in the same saucepan and cook the chicken for about 5 minutes, turning frequently. Season and return the onion mixture to the pan along with the chopped ginger.

5. Blend the milk and cornflour and stir into the chicken mixture. Bring to the boil and stir until very thick. Mix in the soured cream and cook gently to heat through. Do not boil.

6. Heat the taco shells on a baking sheet in an oven preheated to 180°C/350°F/Gas Mark 4, for 2-3 minutes. Place on the sheet with the open ends down.

7. To fill, hold the shell in one hand and spoon in about 1 tbsp of either the beef or chicken filling.

8. Next, add a layer of shredded lettuce, followed by a layer of grated cheese.

9. Add choice of other toppings and finally spoon on some taco sauce.

TIME: Preparation takes about 40 minutes. Cooking takes about 20 minutes.

FLAUTAS

Traditionally, these are long, thin rolls of tortillas with savoury fillings, topped with soured cream.

SERVES 6

225g/8oz chicken, skinned, boned and minced or finely chopped
1 tbsp oil
1 small onion, finely chopped
½ green pepper, finely chopped
½-1 chilli, seeded and finely chopped
90g/3oz frozen sweetcorn, defrosted
6 black olives, pitted and chopped
120ml/4 fl oz double cream
Salt
12 prepared tortillas (see recipe for Flour Tortillas)
Taco Sauce, Guacamole and soured cream, for toppings

1. Use a food processor to prepare the chicken, or chop by hand.

2. Heat the oil in a medium frying pan and add the chicken, onion and green pepper. Cook over a moderate heat, stirring frequently to break up the pieces of chicken.

3. When the chicken is cooked and the vegetables are softened, add the chilli, sweetcorn, olives, cream and salt. Bring to the boil over a high heat and boil rapidly, stirring continuously to reduce and thicken the cream.

4. Place 2 tortillas on a clean work surface, overlapping them by about 5cm/2 inches. Spoon some of the chicken mixture onto the tortillas, roll up and secure with wooden cocktail sticks.

5. Fry the flautas in about 1.25cm/½ inch oil in a large frying pan. Do not allow the tortillas to get very brown. Drain on kitchen paper.

6. Arrange the flautas on serving plates and top with soured cream, guacamole and taco sauce.

TIME: Preparation takes about 1 hour for the tortillas and about 30 minutes to finish the dish.

VARIATION: Use pork or beef in place of the chicken. Green olives may be substituted for black, and red peppers for green.

SERVING IDEAS: Flautas are often served with rice, refried beans and a salad.

CHILLI CON CARNE

Although this dish is Mexican in origin, the version everyone knows best is really more American.

SERVES 4

1 tbsp oil
460g/1lb minced beef
2 tsps ground cumin
2 tsps mild or hot chilli powder
Pinch oregano
Salt, pepper and pinch sugar
¼ tsp garlic powder
2 tbsps flour
460g/1lb canned tomatoes
460g/1lb canned red kidney beans
Boiled rice, to serve

1. Heat the oil in a large saucepan and brown the meat, breaking it up with a fork as it cooks.

2. Sprinkle on the cumin, chilli powder, oregano, salt, pepper and sugar, garlic and flour. Cook, stirring frequently, over a medium heat for about 3 minutes.

3. Add the tomatoes and their liquid and simmer for 25-30 minutes.

4. Drain the kidney beans and add just before serving, heating through for about 5 minutes.

TIME: Preparation takes about 15 minutes. Cooking takes about 10 minutes to brown the meat and 25-30 minutes to cook after the tomatoes are added.

SERVING IDEAS: Spoon the chilli on top of boiled rice to serve. Top with a combination of soured cream, chopped onion, grated cheese and diced avocado. Accompany with tortillas.

TO FREEZE: Allow the chilli to cool completely and place in rigid containers, seal, label and freeze for up to 3 months. Thaw completely before reheating.

CHICKEN NUEVA MEXICANA

SERVES 6

6 chicken thighs, skinned and boned
2 tbsps mild chilli powder
2 tbsps oil
Juice of 1 lime

Lime cream sauce
175ml/6 fl oz soured cream
1 tsp lime juice and grated zest
90ml/6 tbsps double cream

Corn crêpes
150g/5oz fine yellow cornmeal
60g/2oz flour
Pinch salt
1 whole egg and 1 egg yolk
1 tbsp oil or melted butter or margarine
340ml/12 fl oz milk

Garden salsa
1 large courgette, diced
2 shallots, diced
1 large ripe tomato, skinned and diced
1 tbsp chopped fresh coriander
Pinch cayenne pepper and salt
1 tbsp white wine vinegar
3 tbsps oil

Avocado and orange salad
1 avocado, peeled and sliced
2 oranges, peeled and segmented
Juice of 1 lime
Pinch sugar and coriander
45g/6 tbsps pine nuts, toasted

1. Put the chicken in a dish. Combine the chilli powder, oil, lime juice and a pinch of salt and pour over. Cover and refrigerate for 2 hours.

2. Combine the ingredients for the Lime sauce and fold together. Cover and chill for 2 hours.

3. Sift the cornmeal, flour and salt for the crêpes into a bowl. Combine the eggs, oil and milk, add to the bowl and stir to incorporate the dry ingredients. Leave to stand for 30 minutes.

4. Combine the salsa ingredients, cover and leave to marinate.

5. Heat some oil in a frying pan and add the chicken in a single layer. Fry quickly to brown both sides. Pour in the marinade, cover and cook for 25 minutes, or until tender.

6. Heat some oil in a crêpe pan. Wipe out with kitchen paper and return to the heat. Pour in a spoonful of batter and swirl to coat the bottom of the pan. When the edges of the crêpe look pale brown and the top begins to bubble, turn it over and cook the other side. Stack up, cover with foil and keep warm.

7. Combine all the salad ingredients, except the pine nuts, and toss gently.

8. To serve, place one crêpe on a plate. Place a piece of chicken on half of the crêpe, top with some lime sauce, then place some salsa and salad on either side of the chicken and partially fold the crêpe over the top. Scatter over the pine nuts.

PRAWNS VERACRUZ

Veracruz is a port on the Gulf of Mexico which lends its name to a variety of colourful seafood dishes.

SERVES 6

1 tbsp oil
1 onion, chopped
1 large green pepper, cut into 4cm/1½-inch
   strips
2-3 green chillies, seeded and chopped
Double quantity Taco Sauce recipe
2 tomatoes, skinned and roughly chopped
12 pimento-stuffed olives, halved
2 tsps capers
¼ ground cumin
Salt
460g/1lb raw, peeled prawns, uncooked
Juice of 1 lime
Boiled rice, to serve

1. Heat the oil in a large frying pan and add the onion and green pepper. Cook until soft but not coloured.

2. Add the chillies, taco sauce, tomatoes, olives, capers, cumin and salt. Bring to the boil and then lower the heat to simmer for 5 minutes.

3. Remove the black veins, if present, from the rounded side of the prawns with a cocktail stick.

4. Add the prawns to the sauce and cook until they curl up and turn pink and opaque. Add the lime juice to taste and serve with boiled rice.

TIME: Preparation takes about 25 minutes and cooking takes about 15 minutes.

PREPARATION: The sauce may be prepared in advance and reheated while cooking the prawns.

VARIATION: If using cooked prawns, reheat for about 5 minutes. Do not overcook.

BARBECUED PORK STEW

*Named for the sauce rather than the cooking method, this stew requires long,
slow cooking to bring out its flavour.*

SERVES 4

2 tbsps oil
900g/2lb pork shoulder, cut in 5cm/2-inch
   cubes
2 medium onions, cut in 5cm/2-inch pieces
1 large green pepper, cut in 5cm/2-inch
   pieces
1 tbsp chilli powder
2 cloves garlic, crushed
460g/1lb canned tomatoes
3 tbsps tomato purée
1 tbsp Worcestershire sauce
120ml/4 fl oz beef stock
2 tbsps cider vinegar
1 bay leaf
½ tsp dried oregano
Salt and a few drops Tabasco

1. Heat the oil in a large frying pan. When hot, add the pork cubes in two batches. Brown over a high heat for about 5 minutes per batch. Remove to a plate. Add more oil if necessary and cook the onions and pepper to soften slightly. Add the chilli powder and garlic and cook for 1 minute more.

2. Add the tomatoes, their juice and the tomato purée. Stir in the Worcestershire sauce, stock and vinegar, breaking up the tomatoes slightly. Add the bay leaf, oregano and salt.

3. Transfer to a flameproof casserole dish. Bring the mixture to the boil, cover and then cook slowly for about 1½ hours.

4. When the meat is completely tender, skim any fat from the surface of the sauce, remove the bay leaf and add a few drops of Tabasco to taste. Adjust the seasoning and serve.

TIME: Preparation takes about 25 minutes and cooking takes about
1½ hours.

TO FREEZE: Allow the stew to cool completely. Spoon into freezer
containers, cover tightly and freeze for up to 3 months. Defrost in the
refrigerator and then slowly bring to the boil to re-heat before serving.

SERVING IDEAS: Accompany with warm tortillas and serve Spicy Rice and
Beans as a side dish.

MINUTE STEAKS WITH TACO SAUCE

A quick meal needn't be ordinary. Prepare the taco sauce ahead and keep it on hand to add last-minute spice to a meal.

SERVES 6

Full quantity Taco Sauce recipe
30g/1oz butter or margarine
2 tbsps oil
6 minute steaks
Salt and pepper
120g/4oz button mushrooms, left whole
Chopped parsley or coriander leaves

1. Prepare the taco sauce according to the recipe. Heat the butter and oil together in a large frying pan.

2. Season the steaks with salt and pepper and fry two or three at a time for 2-3 minutes on each side, or to taste.

3. Remove the steaks to a warm serving dish and add the mushrooms to the pan. Sauté over a high heat to brown lightly, remove and keep warm.

4. Drain most of the fat from the pan and pour in the taco sauce. Place over a low heat until just bubbling. Spoon over the steaks.

5. Top the steaks with the sautéed mushrooms and sprinkle over some parsley or coriander before serving.

TIME: Preparation takes about 15 minutes. Cooking takes 4-6 minutes per batch of steaks and about 10 minutes more to finish off the dish.

VARIATION: Substitute turkey escalopes for the steaks, if wished, and cook until the juices run clear.

SERVING IDEAS: Serve with rice or flour tortillas.

Swordfish with Grapefruit Tequila Salsa

Rich and dense in texture, swordfish takes very well to a tart grapefruit accompaniment with a dash of tequila.

SERVES 4

Juice of 1 lime
2 tbsps oil
Black pepper to taste
4-8 swordfish steaks (depending on size)
Coriander sprigs, for garnish

Grapefruit salsa
4-6 ruby or pink grapefruit (depending on size)
1 lime
½ a green chilli, seeded and finely diced
1 spring onion, finely chopped
2 tbsps chopped fresh coriander
1 tbsp sugar
3 tbsps tequila

1. To prepare the salsa, remove the zest from the grapefruit and lime with a zester and set it aside.

2. Remove all the pith from the grapefruit and segment them. Squeeze the lime for juice. Mix the grapefruit segments and the two zests with the chilli, onion, coriander, sugar, tequila and lime juice and set aside.

3. Mix the other measure of lime juice, together with the oil and pepper and brush on to both sides of the fish. Place under a preheated grill and cook for about 4 minutes each side depending on distance from the heat source.

4. To serve, place a coriander sprig on each fish steak and serve with the grapefruit salsa.

TIME: Preparation takes about 35 minutes and cooking takes about 8-10 minutes.

PREPARATION: The amount of sugar needed will vary depending on the sweetness of the grapefruit.

COOK'S TIP: For extra flavour, the swordfish steaks may be marinated in the lime juice and oil mixture for up to 1 hour.

CHILLI VERDE

A chilli is really a spicy meat stew. This one is made with pork and given extra flavour with beer.

SERVES 6-8

60ml/4 tbsps oil
900g/2lbs lean pork, cut into 2.5cm/1-inch pieces
3 green peppers, cut into 2.5cm/1-inch pieces
1-2 green chillies, seeded and finely chopped
1 small bunch spring onions, chopped
2 cloves garlic, crushed
2 tsps ground cumin
2 tsps chopped fresh oregano
3 tbsps chopped fresh coriander
1 bay leaf
700ml/1¼ pints beer, water or chicken stock
225g/8oz canned chickpeas, drained
1½ tbsps cornflour mixed with 3 tbsps cold water (optional)
Salt
1 large ripe avocado, peeled and diced
1 tbsp lime juice

1. Heat the oil in a large flameproof casserole and lightly brown the pork cubes in two or three batches over a high heat.

2. Lower the heat and cook the peppers to soften slightly. Add the chillies, onions, garlic and cumin and cook for 2 minutes.

3. Add the herbs and liquid and reduce the heat. Simmer, covered, for 1-1½ hours or until the meat is tender. Add the chickpeas during the last 45 minutes.

4. If necessary, thicken with the cornflour mixture, stirring constantly after adding until the liquid thickens and clears.

5. Add salt to taste and remove the bay leaf.

6. Toss the avocado in the lime juice and sprinkle over the top of the chilli to serve.

TIME: Preparation takes about 30-40 minutes and cooking takes about 1-1½ hours.

VARIATION: Vary the amount of chillies, garlic and herbs to suit your own taste.

SERVING IDEAS: Serve with warm tortillas and boiled rice.

CHILLI RELLENOS

Organization is the key to preparing these stuffed peppers which are fried in a light batter coating until golden.

SERVES 4

Full quantity Red Sauce (see recipe for
    Chalupas)
8 small green peppers
4 small green chillies, seeded and finely
    chopped
1 clove garlic, crushed
1 tsp chopped fresh sage
225g/8oz cream cheese
225g/8oz grated mild cheese
Salt
Flour, for dredging
Oil, for deep frying
8 eggs, separated
45g/6 tbsps plain flour
Pinch salt
Finely chopped spring onions

1. Blanch the whole peppers in boiling water for about 10-15 minutes, or until just tender. Rinse them in cold water and pat them dry.

2. Carefully cut around the stems to make a lid, remove and set aside. Scoop out the seeds and cores, leaving the peppers whole. Leave upside down on kitchen paper to drain.

3. Mix together the chillies, garlic, sage, cheeses and salt to taste. Fill the peppers using a teaspoon and replace the tops, sticking them into the filling.

4. Dredge the peppers with flour and heat the oil in a deep fat fryer to 190°C/375°F.

5. Beat the egg yolks and flour in a mixing bowl until the mixture forms a ribbon trail when the beaters are lifted.

6. Beat the whites with a pinch of salt until stiff but not dry. Fold into the egg yolk mixture.

7. Shape 2 tbsps of batter into an oval and drop into the oil. Immediately slide a metal draining spoon under the batter to hold it in place. Place on a filled pepper. Cover the tops of the peppers with more batter and then spoon over hot oil to seal. Fry until the batter is brown on all sides, turning the peppers over carefully.

8. Drain on kitchen paper and keep them warm on a rack in a moderate oven while frying the remaining peppers.

9. Sprinkle with onions and serve with the Red Sauce.

TIME: Preparation takes about 40 minutes and cooking takes about 3 minutes per pepper. Red Sauce will take about 15 minutes to cook.

COOK'S TIP: Sprinkling savoury foods lightly with salt helps to draw out any excess oil. For fried sweet foods, substitute sugar.

SERVING IDEAS: Chilli Rellenos may be served as a main course with a salad and Refried Beans. These also make a good starter for 8 served with either the Red Sauce, Mole Verde or Garden Salsa.

LEG OF LAMB WITH CHILLI SAUCE

Give Sunday roast lamb a completely different taste with a spicy orange sauce.

SERVES 4

1kg/2¼lb leg of lamb
Orange slices and coriander, to garnish

Marinade
1 tsp cocoa powder
¼ tsp cayenne pepper
½ tsp ground cumin
½ tsp paprika
½ tsp ground oregano
120ml/4 fl oz water
120ml/4 fl oz orange juice
120ml/4 fl oz red wine
1 clove of garlic, crushed
2 tbsps brown sugar
Pinch of salt
1 tbsp cornflour

---

1. If the lamb has a lot of surface fat, trim slightly with a sharp knife. If possible, remove the paper-thin skin on the outside of the lamb. Place lamb in a shallow dish.

2. Mix together the marinade ingredients, except the cornflour, and pour over the lamb, turning it well to coat completely. Cover and refrigerate for 12-24 hours, turning occasionally.

3. Drain the lamb, reserving the marinade, and place in a roasting tin. Cook in an oven preheated to 180°C/350°F/Gas Mark 4, for about 1¾-2 hours, or until meat is cooked according to taste.

4. Baste occasionally with the marinade and pan juices.

5. Remove the lamb to a serving dish and keep warm. Skim the fat from the top of the roasting tin with a large spoon and discard.

6. Pour the remaining marinade into the pan juices in the roasting tin and bring to the boil, stirring. Mix the cornflour with a small amount of water and add some of the liquid from the roasting tin. Gradually stir the cornflour mixture into the tin and bring back to the boil.

7. Cook, stirring constantly, until thickened and clear. Add more orange juice, wine or water as necessary.

8. Garnish the lamb with the orange slices and sprigs of coriander. Pour over some of the sauce and serve the rest separately.

TIME: Preparation takes about 15 minutes, with 12-24 hours for the lamb to marinate. Cooking takes about 1¾-2 hours for the lamb and 20 minutes to finish the sauce.

COOK'S TIP: The marinade ingredients can also be used with beef or poultry.

SERVING IDEAS: Serve with rice or boiled potatoes and vegetables.

CHICKEN WITH RED PEPPERS

Easy as this recipe is, it makes excellent fare for a dinner party. Serve with boiled rice and vegetables.

SERVES 4

4 large red peppers
4 skinned and boned chicken breasts
1½ tbsps oil
Salt and pepper
1 clove garlic, finely chopped
3 tbsps white wine vinegar
2 spring onions, finely chopped
Sage leaves, for garnish

1. Cut the peppers in half and remove the stems, cores and seeds. Flatten the peppers with the palm of your hand and brush the skin sides lightly with oil.

2. Place the peppers skin side up on the rack of a pre-heated grill and cook about 5cm/2 inches away from the heat source until the skins are well blistered and charred.

3. Wrap the peppers in a clean tea-towel and allow them to stand until cool. Peel off the skins with a small vegetable knife and cut the flesh into thin strips.

4. Place the chicken breasts between two sheets of dampened greaseproof paper and flatten by hitting with a rolling pin or meat mallet.

5. Heat the oil in a large frying pan. Season the chicken breasts on both sides and add to the pan. Cook for 5 minutes, turn over and cook until tender and lightly browned. Remove the chicken and keep it warm.

6. Add the pepper strips, garlic, vinegar and spring onions to the pan and cook briefly until the vinegar loses its strong aroma.

7. Slice the chicken breasts across the grain into 5mm/¼-inch thick slices and arrange on serving places. Spoon over the pan juices.

8. Arrange the pepper mixture with the chicken and garnish with the sage leaves.

TIME: Preparation takes about 35-40 minutes and cooking takes about 10 minutes to char the peppers and about 20 minutes to finish the dish.

VARIATION: For convenience, the dish may be prepared with canned pimento caps instead of red peppers. These will be softer so cook the garlic, vinegar and onions to soften, and then add pimento.

PLAICE WITH SPICY TOMATO SAUCE

This piquant fish dish is popular along Mexico's Gulf coast.

SERVES 4

90g/3oz cream cheese
1 tsp dried oregano
Pinch of cayenne pepper
4 whole fillets of plaice, skinned
Lime slices and dill, to garnish

Tomato sauce
1 tbsp oil
1 small onion, chopped
1 stick celery, chopped
1 chilli, seeded and chopped
¼ tsp each ground cumin, coriander and
    ginger
½ red and ½ green pepper, chopped
400g/14oz can tomatoes
1 tbsp tomato purée
Salt, pepper and a pinch of sugar

1. To prepare the sauce, heat the oil in a heavy-based pan and cook the onion, celery, chilli and spices for about 5 minutes over a very low heat.

2. Add the peppers and the remaining sauce ingredients and bring to the boil. Reduce the heat and simmer for 15-20 minutes, stirring occasionally. Set aside while preparing the fish.

3. Mix the cream cheese, oregano and cayenne pepper together and set aside.

4. Spread the cheese filling on all 4 fish fillets and roll each up. Secure with wooden cocktail sticks.

5. Place the fillets in a lightly greased baking dish, cover and cook for 10 minutes in an oven preheated to 180°C/350°F/Gas Mark 4.

6. Pour over the tomato sauce and cook for a further 10-15 minutes, or until the fish feels firm and looks opaque. Garnish with lime slices and dill.

TIME: Preparation takes about 30 minutes and cooking takes 20-25 minutes.

SERVING IDEAS: Accompany with rice and an avocado salad.

VARIATION: Add prawns or crabmeat to the filling for a dinner party dish.

CHILLI ROJA

*Red meat, red onions, red peppers, paprika, tomatoes and red beans all give clues
to the name of this zesty stew.*

SERVES 6-8

Oil
900g/2lbs beef chuck steak, cut into
    2.5cm/1-inch pieces
1 large red onion, coarsely chopped
2 cloves garlic, crushed
2 red peppers, cut into 2.5cm/1-inch pieces
1-2 red chillies, seeded and finely chopped
3 tbsps mild chilli powder
1 tbsp cumin
1 tbsp paprika
700ml/1¼ pints beer, water or stock
225g/8oz canned tomatoes, puréed
2 tbsps tomato purée
225g/8oz canned red kidney beans, drained
Pinch of salt
6 ripe tomatoes, skinned, seeded and diced

1. Pour about 60ml/4 tbsps oil into a large saucepan or flameproof casserole. When hot, brown the meat in small batches over a moderately high heat for about 5 minutes per batch.

2. Set aside the meat on a plate or in the lid of the casserole. Lower the heat and cook the onion, garlic, red peppers and chillies for about 5 minutes. Add the chilli powder, cumin and paprika and cook for a further minute. Pour on the liquid and add the canned tomatoes, tomato purée and the meat.

3. Cook slowly for about 1½-2 hours. Add the beans about 45 minutes before the end of cooking time.

4. When the meat is completely tender, add salt to taste and serve garnished with the diced tomatoes.

TIME: Preparation takes about 25 minutes and cooking takes about
1½-2 hours.

TO FREEZE: The chilli may be frozen for up to 3 months in a tightly covered freezer container. Allow the chilli to cool completely before sealing and freezing. Defrost in the refrigerator and bring slowly to the boil before serving.

VARIATION: The chilli may be made with pork shoulder or with a mixture of beef and pork. Although not authentic, the chilli may also be made with ground beef or pork.

Spare Ribs in Chilli & Cream Sauce

Cocoa powder lends colour and depth to a sauce for ribs that's slightly more sophisticated than the usual barbecue sauce.

SERVES 4

1kg/2¼lbs pork spare ribs, in racks
1 tsp cocoa powder
1 tbsp flour
½ tsp cumin
½ tsp paprika
¼-½ tsp chilli powder
½ tsp dried oregano, crushed
Salt and pepper
225ml/8 fl oz warm water
2 tbsps liquid honey
2 tbsps double cream
Lime wedges and watercress, for garnish

1. Leave the ribs in whole slabs and roast in an oven preheated to 200°C/400°F/Gas Mark 6, for 20-25 minutes, or until well browned. Drain off all the excess fat.

2. Blend together the cocoa, flour, cumin, paprika, chilli powder, oregano, seasoning, water and honey and pour over the ribs. Lower the temperature to 180°C/350°F/Gas Mark 4 and cook the ribs for a further 30 minutes, until the sauce has reduced and the ribs are tender.

3. Cut the ribs into pieces and arrange on a serving dish.

4. Pour the cream into the sauce in the roasting tin and place over a moderate heat. Bring to the boil and pour over the ribs.

5. Garnish with lime wedges and watercress to serve.

TIME: Preparation takes about 20 minutes, cooking takes 50-55 minutes.

PREPARATION: Ribs may be cooked for the last 30 minutes on an outdoor barbecue grill.

SERVING IDEAS: Serve with rice and an avocado or tomato salad.

CHILLI WITH THREE BEANS

Although often called a soup, this dish is so hearty that it is really a complete meal in itself.

SERVES 6

---

3 tbsps vegetable oil
2 medium onions, roughly chopped
1 clove garlic, crushed
1 tbsp ground cumin
2 tsps paprika pepper
1 red or green chilli, seeded and chopped
680g/1½lbs minced beef
800g/1¾lbs canned tomatoes
90g/3oz tomato purée
1 tsp oregano
1 bay leaf
140ml/¼ pint beer
Salt and pepper
120g/4oz each of canned and drained red
    kidney beans, white kidney beans, pinto
    beans and chickpeas

1. Heat the oil in a large pan. Add the onions and cook gently until soft but not browned.

2. Add the garlic, cumin, paprika and chilli. Cook for 1 minute, before stirring in the beef.

3. Cook the meat until it is lightly browned, breaking it up with a fork to prevent large lumps forming.

4. Stir in the tomatoes and their juice, the tomato purée, oregano, bay leaf and beer. Season to taste, then cover and simmer for 50 minutes. Check the level of liquid several times during cooking and add a little water if necessary.

5. Fifteen minutes before the end of the cooking time, stir in the drained beans and chickpeas.

TIME: Preparation takes 30 minutes, and cooking takes about 1 hour.

PREPARATION: This soup can be prepared in advance and reheated.

SERVING IDEAS: Serve the soup with corn or tortilla chips and a garnish of soured cream, grated cheese, diced avocado, or chopped spring onions.

TO FREEZE: This soup can be frozen for up to three months.

RIVERSIDE TROUT

Trout is so delicious that simple preparation is all that's necessary. Crisp cornmeal, bacon and pine nuts complement the fresh flavour.

SERVES 4

30g/4 tbsps pine nuts
Vegetable oil, for frying
8 rashers bacon, diced
150g/5oz yellow cornmeal
Pinch salt and white pepper
4 trout weighing about 225g/8oz each,
  cleaned
Juice of 1 lime
Fresh sage or coriander, to garnish

1. Heat a large frying pan. Add the pine nuts and dry-toast over a moderate heat, stirring constantly. When a pale golden brown, remove them with a draining spoon to kitchen paper.

2. Add a little oil to the pan, and cook the diced bacon until crisp, stirring constantly. Drain with the pine nuts.

3. Mix the cornmeal, salt and pepper, and dredge the fish well, patting on the cornmeal. Shake off any excess.

4. Add more oil to the pan – it should come about halfway up the sides of the fish. Re-heat over moderately high heat.

5. When hot, add the fish two at a time and fry until golden brown, about 4-5 minutes. Turn over and reduce the heat slightly if necessary and cook a further 4-5 minutes. Drain and repeat with the remaining fish.

6. Drain almost all the oil from the pan and re-heat the bacon and the nuts very briefly. Add the lime juice and cook for a few seconds. Spoon the bacon and pine nut mixture over the fish and garnish with coriander or sage.

TIME: Preparation takes about 25 minutes and cooking takes about 15-20 minutes.

PREPARATION: When coating fish, seafood or chicken with flour or cornmeal, prepare just before ready to cook. If the food stands with its coating for too long before cooking, the coating will become soggy.

VARIATION: If wished, the trout may be dredged with plain or wholewheat flour instead of the cornmeal.

SPICY CHICKEN

Chillies, coriander and tomatoes add warm Mexican flavour to grilled chicken.

SERVES 6

6 boned chicken breasts
Grated zest and juice of 1 lime
2 tbsps olive oil
Coarsely ground black pepper
90ml/6 tbsps whole grain mustard
2 tsps paprika
4 ripe tomatoes, skinned, seeded and
    quartered
2 shallots, chopped
1 clove garlic, crushed
½ Jalapeño pepper or other chilli, seeded
    and chopped
1 tsp wine vinegar
Pinch of salt
2 tbsps chopped fresh coriander
Whole coriander leaves, to garnish

1. Place the chicken breasts in a shallow dish with the lime zest and juice, oil, pepper, mustard and paprika. Marinate for about 1 hour, turning occasionally.

2. To skin the tomatoes easily, drop them into boiling water for about 20 seconds or less depending on ripeness. Place immediately in cold water. The skins should come off easily.

3. Place the tomatoes, shallots, garlic, chilli, vinegar and salt in a food processor or blender and process until coarsely chopped. Stir in the coriander by hand.

4. Place the chicken on a grill pan and reserve the marinade. Cook the chicken skin side uppermost for about 7-10 minutes, depending on how close the chicken is to the heat source. Baste frequently with the remaining marinade. Grill the other side in the same way. Sprinkle with salt after grilling.

5. Place the chicken on serving plates and garnish the top with coriander leaves or sprigs. Serve with a spoonful of the tomato salsa on one side.

TIME: Preparation takes about 1 hour and cooking takes 14-20 minutes.

PREPARATION: The tomato salsa can be prepared in advance and kept in the refrigerator. It can also be served with meat or seafood and makes a good dip for vegetable crudités or tortilla chips.

WATCHPOINT: When preparing chillies wear rubber gloves or at least be sure to wash hands thoroughly after handling them. Do not touch eyes or face before washing hands.

ALBONDIGAS (MEATBALLS)

A simple-to-make taco sauce makes plain meatballs a lot less ordinary and a lot more fun to eat.

SERVES 4

225g/8oz ground veal
225g/8oz ground beef
1 clove garlic, crushed
2 tbsps dry breadcrumbs
½ chilli, seeded and finely chopped
½ tsp ground cumin
Salt and pepper
1 egg, beaten
3 tbsps oil
Full quantity Taco Sauce recipe
2 spring onions, chopped

1. Mix together the veal, beef, garlic, breadcrumbs, chilli, cumin and salt and pepper until well blended. Add the egg gradually.

2. Turn the mixture out onto a floured surface and divide into 16 equal pieces.

3. With floured hands, shape the mixture into balls.

4. Pour the oil into a large frying pan and place over high heat.

5. When the oil is hot, place in the meatballs and fry for 5-10 minutes until brown on all sides. Turn frequently during cooking.

6. Remove the browned meatballs and drain well on kitchen paper. Place in an ovenproof dish and pour over the taco sauce.

7. Heat through in an oven preheated to 180°C/350°F/Gas Mark 4, for 10 minutes. Sprinkle with chopped spring onions to serve.

TIME: Preparation takes about 25 minutes and cooking time about 20 minutes.

SERVING IDEAS: Serve with rice, refried beans or guacamole. Drizzle with soured cream if wished.

TO FREEZE: Prepare and cook the meatballs and allow to cool completely. Place the meatballs on baking sheets and place in the freezer until firm. Transfer to freezer containers, label and store for up to 3 months. Defrost in the refrigerator and reheat according to the recipe.

SPICY RICE AND BEANS

A lively side dish or vegetarian main course, this recipe readily takes to creative variations and even makes a good cold salad.

SERVES 6-8

60ml/4 tbsps oil
400g/14oz long grain rice
1 onion, finely chopped
1 green pepper, chopped
1 tsp each ground cumin and coriander
1-2 tsps Tabasco
Salt
850ml/1½ pints stock
460g/1lb canned red kidney beans, drained
  and rinsed
460g/1lb canned tomatoes, drained and
  coarsely chopped
Chopped parsley

1. Heat the oil in a casserole or a large, deep saucepan.

2. Add the rice and cook until just turning opaque. Add the onion, pepper and cumin and coriander. Cook gently for a further 2 minutes.

3. Add the Tabasco, salt, stock and beans and bring to the boil. Cover and cook for about 45 minutes, or until the rice is tender and most of the liquid is absorbed.

4. Remove from the heat and add the tomatoes, stirring them in gently. Leave to stand, covered, for 5 minutes.

5. Fluff up the mixture with a fork and sprinkle with parsley to serve.

TIME: Preparation takes about 25 minutes and cooking takes about 50 minutes.

SERVING IDEAS: Serve with warm tortillas and a salad for a light vegetarian meal. Serve as a side dish with enchiladas, meat or poultry, or cheese and egg dishes.

VARIATION: The recipe may be made with fresh tomatoes, skinned, seeded and coarsely chopped.

ROAST PEPPER SALAD

Charring the peppers makes the skins easier to remove and gives a slightly smoky taste that is very pleasant.

SERVES 6

6 red peppers
90ml/6 tbsps olive oil
2 tbsps red or white wine vinegar
Salt and pepper
1 clove garlic, roughly chopped
1 spring onion, diagonally sliced

1. Preheat a grill and cut the peppers in half, removing the seeds, stems and cores.

2. Flatten the peppers with the palm of your hand and brush the skin side of each pepper lightly with oil. Place the peppers on the grill rack under the grill.

3. Grill the peppers until the skins are well charred on top. Do not turn the peppers over.

4. Wrap the peppers in a clean towel and leave to stand for about 15-20 minutes.

5. Unwrap the peppers and peel off the skin using a small, sharp knife. Cut the peppers into strips or into 2.5cm/1 inch pieces.

6. Mix the remaining oil with the vinegar, salt and pepper. Place the peppers in a serving dish and pour over the dressing.

7. Sprinkle over the garlic and spring onion and leave the peppers to stand for about 30 minutes before serving.

TIME: Preparation takes about 20 minutes. Grilling time for the peppers is about 10-12 minutes.

PREPARATION: The peppers must be well charred for the skin to loosen easily. Wrapping peppers in a tea-towel creates steam, which helps to loosen the skin more easily.

SERVING IDEAS: Serve as a starter or mix with cooked cold rice for a more substantial salad.

FRIJOLES REFRITOS (REFRIED BEANS)

This is a classic accompaniment to Mexican main courses be they poultry or meat, vegetable or cheese.

SERVES 6-8

225g/8oz dried pinto beans
Water to cover
1 bay leaf
90ml/6 tbsps oil
Salt and pepper
Grated mild cheese
Shredded lettuce
Tortillas

1. Soak the beans overnight in plenty of cold water. Alternatively, bring the beans to the boil in cold water and then allow to boil rapidly for 10 minutes. Cover and leave to stand for one hour. Change the water, add the bay leaf and bring to the boil. Cover and simmer for about 2 hours, or until the beans are completely tender. Drain the beans and reserve a small amount of the cooking liquid. Discard the bay leaf.

2. Heat the oil in a heavy-based frying pan. Add the beans and, as they fry, mash them with the back of a spoon. Do not overmash – about a third of the beans should stay whole. Season to taste.

3. Smooth out the beans in the pan and cook until the bottom is set but not browned. Turn the beans over and cook the other side.

4. Top with some grated cheese and cook the beans until the cheese melts. Serve with finely shredded lettuce and warm tortillas, or tortilla chips.

TIME: Preparation takes about 15 minutes. The beans must be soaked overnight or rehydrated by the quick method. The beans must be cooked at least 2 hours before frying.

WATCHPOINT: Make sure the beans are completely tender and have boiled rapidly for at least 45 minutes before eating.

SERVING IDEAS: Serve the beans as a side dish with enchiladas or with barbecued meats.

Taco Sauce

This basic recipe has many uses in Mexican cooking – sauce, topping, dip or as an ingredient to give a dish extra flavour.

MAKES 280ml/½ pint

1 tbsp oil
1 onion, diced
1 green pepper, diced
½-1 red or green chilli
½ tsp ground cumin
½ tsp ground coriander
½ clove garlic, crushed
Pinch of salt, pepper and sugar
400g/14oz can tomatoes
Tomato purée (optional)

1. Heat the oil in a heavy-based saucepan and when hot, add the onion and pepper. Cook slowly to soften slightly.

2. Chop the chilli and add with the cumin, coriander, garlic and cook a further 2-3 minutes.

3. Add sugar, seasonings and the tomatoes with their juice.

4. Cook for a further 5-6 minutes over a moderate heat to reduce and thicken slightly. Add the tomato purée for colour, if necessary. Adjust the seasoning and use hot or cold according to your recipe.

TIME: Preparation takes about 15-20 minutes, cooking takes about 8-10 minutes.

SERVING IDEAS: Use as a sauce or topping for fish, meat or poultry main dishes. Use in tacos, tostadas, nachos and as a dip for tortilla chips or vegetable crudités.

TO FREEZE: Fill rigid containers with the sauce at room temperature. Label and freeze for up to 3 months. Defrost at room temperature, breaking the sauce up as it thaws.

FLOUR TORTILLAS

Tortillas made with wheat instead of corn are traditional in northern Mexico.
Flour tortillas are easier to make and use than the corn variety.

MAKES 12

460g/1lb plain flour
1 tbsp salt
90g/3oz lard or white vegetable fat
225ml/8 fl oz hot water

1. Sift the flour and salt into a mixing bowl and rub in the lard until the mixture resembles fine breadcrumbs. Mix in the water gradually to form a soft, pliable dough.

2. Knead on a well-floured surface until smooth and no longer sticky. Cover with a damp tea-towel.

3. Cut off about 3 tbsps of dough at a time, keeping the rest covered. Knead into a ball.

4. Roll the ball of dough out into a very thin circle with a floured rolling pin. Cut into a neat round using a 25cm/10 inch plate as a guide. Continue until all the dough is used.

5. Stack the tortillas as you make them, flouring each well to prevent sticking. Cover with a clean tea-towel.

6. Heat a large heavy-based frying pan and carefully place in a tortilla. Cook for about 10 seconds per side. Stack and keep covered until all are cooked. Use according to chosen recipe.

TIME: Preparation takes about 60 minutes to make the dough and roll out all the tortillas, cooking takes about 5 minutes.

SERVING IDEAS: Use with any recipe that calls for tortillas. Also, serve hot as an accompaniment to any Mexican dish.

TO FREEZE: Tortillas can be prepared and cooked in advance and frozen. Stack the tortillas between sheets of non-stick or wax paper. Place in plastic bags, seal, label and freeze for up to 2 months. Defrost at room temperature before using.

RED PEPPER RELISH

This sweet but hot and spicy condiment adds a bright spot of colour and flavour to a main course or starter.

MAKES 420ml/¾ pint

5 red peppers, seeded
3 red or green chillies, seeded
340g/12oz sugar
175ml/6 fl oz red wine vinegar
225ml/8 fl oz liquid pectin

1. Chop the peppers and chillies finely in a food processor.

2. Combine the sugar and vinegar in a deep, heavy-based pan and heat gently to dissolve the sugar.

3. Add the peppers and bring the mixture to the boil. Simmer for 15-20 minutes.

4. Stir in the pectin, return the mixture to the boil over a high heat, and cook until the mixture is reduced and the spoon leaves a trail when drawn through the mixture.

5. Pour into sterilized jars, to within about 1.25cm/½-inch of the top. Place a waxed disc, wax down onto the surface of the relish and either cover immediately or leave until it is quite cold before covering with the lids.

TIME: Preparation takes about 20 minutes and cooking takes about 20-25 minutes.

PREPARATION: To sterilize the storage jars heat them in a hot oven for about 15 minutes.

COOK'S TIP: Once a jar of the relish is opened, store it in the refrigerator

SERVING IDEAS: Serve as a condiment with meat, poultry, vegetable, egg or cheese dishes.

Guava Mint Sorbet

When a light dessert is called for, a sorbet can't be surpassed. The exotic taste of guava works well with mint.

MAKES 700ml/1¼ pints

150g/5oz granulated sugar
225ml/8 fl oz water
4 ripe guavas
2 tbsps chopped fresh mint
Juice of 1 lime
1 egg white
Fresh mint leaves, for decoration

1. Combine the sugar and water in a heavy-based saucepan and bring slowly to the boil to dissolve the sugar. When the mixture is a clear syrup, boil rapidly for 30 seconds. Allow to cool to room temperature and then chill in the refrigerator.

2. Cut the guavas in half and scoop out the pulp. Discard the skins and seeds and purée the fruit until smooth in a food processor. Add the mint and combine with the cold syrup. Gradually add the lime juice until the right balance of sweetness is reached.

3. Pour the mixture into a shallow container and freeze until slushy. Process again to break up the ice crystals and then freeze until firm.

4. Whisk the egg white until stiff but not dry. Process the sorbet again and when smooth, fold in the egg white and then freeze again until firm.

5. Remove from the freezer 15 minutes before serving and keep in the refrigerator.

6. Scoop out and decorate each serving with mint leaves.

TIME: Preparation takes about 2-3 hours, allowing the sorbet to freeze between processing.

PREPARATION: If a food processor is not available, use an electric hand mixer.

TO FREEZE: The sorbet will keep in the freezer for up to 3 months in a well-sealed, rigid container.

FRUIT EMPANADAS

Tortillas can have a sweet side, too, when stuffed with cheese and sunny apricots or exotic tropical fruit.

MAKES 10

Oil, for deep frying
Icing sugar

Tortillas
225g/8oz plain flour
2 tsps baking powder
Pinch of salt
60g/2oz white vegetable fat
120-175ml/4-6 fl oz hot water

Filling
10 ripe fresh apricots, halved and pitted, or
    460g/1lb canned apricots, well drained
460g/1lb cream cheese

1. Sift the flour, baking powder and salt into a bowl. Rub in the vegetable fat until the mixture resembles coarse crumbs. Add the water, mixing until it is absorbed. Knead gently and add more flour if the dough is too sticky. Cover and leave to rest for 15 minutes.

2. Divide the dough into ten even-sized pieces. Roll into balls on a floured surface, cover and leave to stand for 20 minutes. Roll out each ball on a lightly floured surface, to a circle 18cm/7 inches in diameter. Cover the finished tortillas whilst rolling all the remaining dough.

3. Heat some oil in a deep saucepan, or deep-fat fryer to a depth of at least 5cm/2 inches. The oil should reach a temperature of 190°C/375°F.

4. Cut the apricots into quarters and the cheese into 10 even pieces. Place one piece of cheese and an even amount of apricots on one half of each tortilla. Fold over the other half and seal the edges. Crimp tightly into a decorative pattern.

5. Fry one empanada at a time until golden on both sides. Baste the upper side frequently with the oil to make the tortillas puffy. Drain well on kitchen paper and serve warm, sprinkled with icing sugar.

TIME: Preparation takes about 40 minutes-1 hour for the tortillas and about 20 minutes to prepare the rest of the dish.

VARIATION: Other fruit may be used in the empanadas instead of apricots. Substitute fresh guava, mango or papaya cut into short strips. Sliced peaches may also be used as well as cherries, although they are not native to Mexico.

PREPARATION: As with all deep-fried foods, fruit empanadas are best served as soon as they are cooked.

CHURROS

These fritters can be sweet or savoury, either way, they're a treat.

MAKES 12-14

Basic dough
225ml/8 fl oz water
45g/1½oz butter or margarine
Pinch of salt
120g/4oz plain flour
60g/6 tbsps cornmeal
2 eggs
Oil, for deep frying

Sweet ingredients
60g/4 tbsps sugar
1 tbsp cocoa powder
1 tsp ground cinnamon
Icing sugar (optional)

Savoury ingredients
2 tbsps finely grated cheese
2 chillies, seeded and finely chopped
Parmesan cheese (optional)

1. Combine the water, butter and salt in a heavy-based saucepan. If making sweet churros, add the sugar as well. Cook over a medium heat until the butter melts.

2. Immediately stir in the flour and cornmeal. Keeping the pan over medium heat, stir until the mixture pulls away from the sides of the pan and forms a ball. Take off the heat and cool slightly.

3. Add the eggs one at a time with the cocoa and cinnamon *or* the cheese and chillies, beating vigorously in between each addition. It may not be necessary to add all the egg. Beat until the mixture is smooth and shiny and thick enough to pipe.

4. Spoon the mixture into a piping bag fitted with a star nozzle.

5. Heat at least 10cm/4 inches of oil in a deep-fat fryer, or deep saucepan. Pipe the dough into the oil in 25.5cm/10-inch strips and fry for about 3 minutes per side, or until golden. Drain on kitchen paper and sprinkle sweet churros with icing sugar, or savoury churros with parmesan cheese if wished. Serve warm.

TIME: Preparation takes about 25-30 minutes and cooking takes about 6 minutes per piece.

PREPARATION: As the churros cook in the hot fat, they will curl into different shapes.

COOK'S TIP: The mixture will be easier to pipe if it is used just after preparation.

MANGO FOOL

To cool the palate after a spicy Mexican meal, the taste of mango, lime, ginger and cream is perfect.

SERVES 6

2 ripe mangoes
1 small piece fresh root ginger, peeled and
    shredded
120g/4oz icing sugar, sifted
Juice of ½ lime
140ml/¼ pint double cream

1. Cut the mangoes in half, cutting either side of the large central stone. Reserve two slices, then scoop out the flesh into a bowl, blender or food processor.

2. Add the ginger, icing sugar and lime juice and purée in the blender or food processor until smooth.

3. Whip the cream until soft peaks form and then fold into the mango purée.

4. Divide the mixture between 6 glass serving dishes and leave in the refrigerator for 1 hour before serving.

5. Cut the reserved mango slices into 6 smaller slices or pieces and use to decorate the fool.

TIME: Preparation takes about 20 minutes. Plus 1 hour chilling time.

SERVING IDEAS: Accompany with crisp biscuits.

WATCHPOINT: When whipping cream, refrigerate it for at least 2 hours before use and be careful not to overwhisk.

TROPICAL FRUIT SALAD

A refreshing mixture of exotic fruits is the most popular sweet in Mexico. Add tequila or triple sec to the syrup for a special occasion.

SERVES 6

½ cantaloup or honeydew melon, cubed or made into balls

½ small fresh pineapple, peeled, cored and cubed or sliced

120g/4oz fresh strawberries, hulled and halved (leave whole, if small)

1 mango, peeled and sliced or cubed

225g/8oz watermelon, seeded and cubed

120g/4oz guava or papaya, peeled and cubed

2 oranges, peeled and segmented

1 prickly pear, peeled and sliced (optional)

120g/4oz caster sugar

120ml/4 fl oz water

Grated zest and juice of 1 lime

2 tbsps chopped pecans, to decorate

1. To make melon balls, cut melons in half and scoop out seeds and discard them. To use a melon baller, press the cutting edge firmly into the melon flesh and twist around to scoop out round pieces.

2. It is easier to core the pineapple if it is first cut into quarters. Use a serrated fruit knife to cut the point off the quarter, removing the core. Slice off the peel and remove any brown 'eyes' with the end of a peeler. Cut into slices or cubes and mix with the other fruit.

3. Dissolve the sugar in the water over gentle heat and when the mixture is no longer grainy, bring to the boil and cook for 1 minute, then leave it to cool completely.

4. Add lime zest and juice to the sugar syrup and pour over the prepared fruit. Refrigerate well before serving, then sprinkle with the chopped nuts.

TIME: Preparation takes about 45 minutes. The syrup will take about 5-7 minutes to make.

PREPARATION: Allow the syrup to cool completely before adding any fruit. Hot syrup will cook the fruit and draw out the juices.

VARIATION: Use other varieties of fruit, choosing whatever is in season.

Mexican Chocolate Flan

Flan in Mexico is a moulded custard with a caramel sauce. Chocolate and cinnamon is a favourite flavour combination.

SERVES 4

120g/4oz caster sugar
2 tbsps water
Juice of ½ lime
60g/2oz plain chocolate
280ml/½ pint milk
1 cinnamon stick
2 whole eggs
2 egg yolks
60g/4 tbsps sugar

1. Combine the first amount of sugar with the water and lime juice in a small, heavy-based saucepan.

2. Cook over a gentle heat, stirring until the sugar dissolves, then without stirring, bring the syrup to the boil and cook until golden brown and caramelized.

3. While preparing the syrup, heat 4 ramekins in an oven preheated to 180°C/350°F/Gas Mark 4. When the syrup is ready, pour into the hot ramekins and swirl to coat the sides and base evenly. Leave to cool at room temperature.

4. Chop the chocolate into small pieces and heat with the milk and cinnamon, stirring occasionally to help the chocolate dissolve.

5. Whisk the whole eggs and the yolks together with the remaining sugar until slightly frothy. Gradually whisk in the hot chocolate milk. Remove the cinnamon stick.

6. Strain the chocolate custard carefully into the ramekins and stand them in a roasting tin filled with enough hand-hot water to come half way up the sides of the dishes.

7. Carefully place the roasting tin in the oven, and bake the custards for 20-25 minutes, or until they have just set, and a knife inserted in the centre of the custard comes out clean.

8. Cool at room temperature and refrigerate for several hours or overnight before serving. Loosen the custards by running a knife around the edges and invert onto individual serving plates. If necessary shake the custard to allow it to drop out.

TIME: Preparation takes about 30 minutes, cooking takes about 35-40 minutes. Plus overnight chilling.

VARIATION: Leave out the chocolate, if wished, for a cinnamon flan.

WATCHPOINT: Do not allow the custard to overcook or it will form a tough skin on top. If the oven temperature is too high, it will cause the custard to boil and spoil the smooth texture.

SERVING IDEAS: Garnish with pecans or chocolate curls. Also good with fruit such as raspberries or bananas (with chocolate flan); peaches or strawberries (with cinnamon flan).

Index